I COULD HAVE DANCED ALL NIGHT

THE GREATEST SONGS OF LERNER & LOEWE

Chappell & Co., Inc.

In early Fall of 1942 at the Lambs Club in N. Y. the legendary collaboration of Alan Jay Lerner and Frederick Loewe commenced with Loewe's direct words: "You are Alan Jay Lerner? You write good lyrics. I'm Frederick Loewe. I would like to talk to you." They joined forces to create a musical for a Detroit, Michigan stock company called *The Life Of The Party,* and though hardly memorable, it was sufficiently encouraging that they essayed a second venture, this time for Broadway. *What's Up* opened in 1943 but lasted only eight weeks. Undaunted, Lerner and Loewe created *The Day Before Spring* in 1946 which delighted theatregoers for six months, however their first smash hit was *Brigadoon* which appeared in 1947. The show was named Best Musical of the Year and Lerner & Loewe were named Best Composer and Best Lyricist by the N. Y. Drama Critics. *Paint Your Wagon* appeared in 1951, and like *Brigadoon,* was a success in both New York and London.

March 15, 1956 is a special night in the annals of theatrical history. It marks the debut of *My Fair Lady,* perhaps the most perfect musical ever written, and in critic Brooks Atkinson's words "one of the best musicals of the century." *My Fair Lady* played 2,717 performances in N. Y., repeated its stupendous success in London, and has triumphed in virtually every major capital of the world. Despite Frederick Loewe's resolve never to write music for a film, Lerner won him over in 1958 and the resultant *Gigi* became another Lerner & Loewe bonanza. The film was voted the Oscar for Best Picture and won more awards than any other in history. With a $2,000,000 advance sale, Lerner and Loewe returned to Broadway in 1960 with *Camelot* which ran two years in N. Y., repeated its success in London, and became a memorable film in 1967.

More recently, Messrs. Loewe and Lerner returned to *Gigi* and converted it to a stage musical which marks their return to Broadway after an absence of more than a decade. Following *Camelot,* Loewe retired to his estate in Palm Springs, while Lerner wrote *On A Clear Day You Can See Forever* and *Coco* plus the screenplays for *Clear Day* and *Paint Your Wagon. Gigi* opened at the Uris Theatre November 13, 1973 and once again Broadway was captivated! 1974 promises a new Lerner & Loewe motion picture, *The Little Prince,* based on the book by Antoine de Saint-Exupery.

When *My Fair Lady* was about to close on Broadway a toast was made to this venerable grande dame which had run so long: "To its taste, its intelligence, its beauty and its bounce." This sentiment is surely one that reflects all the works of Alan Jay Lerner and Frederick Loewe.

CONTENTS

CHERYL CRAWFORD

presents

A NEW MUSICAL

BRIGADOON

Book and Lyrics by
ALAN JAY LERNER

Music by
FREDERICK LOEWE

Dances and Musical Numbers by
AGNES de MILLE

Production Staged by
ROBERT LEWIS

Scenery Designed by
OLIVER SMITH

Costumes Designed by
DAVID FFOLKES

Musical Director FRANZ ALLERS
Orchestrations by TED ROYAL

A Lowal Corporation
Publication.

BROADWAY OPENING MARCH 13, 1947

THE HEATHER ON THE HILL

Music by FREDERICK LOEWE

Lyrics by ALAN JAY LERNER

Can't we two go walk-in' to-geth-er out be-yond the val-ley of trees? Out where there's a hill-side of heath-er curt-sey-in' gent-ly in the breeze That's what I'd like to do; see the heath-er but with you.

REFRAIN

The mist of May is in the gloam-in', and all the clouds are hold-in' still

So take my hand and let's go roam - in' through the

heath-er on the hill. The morn-in'dew is blink-in'

yon - der, there's laz - y mu-sic in the rill,

And all I want to do is wan-der through the heath-er on the hill. There may be

THERE BUT FOR YOU GO I

Music by FREDERICK LOEWE

Lyrics by ALAN JAY LERNER

This is hard to say, but as I wandered through the lea I felt for just a fleet-ing mo-ment that I sud-den-ly was free of be-ing lone-ly; Then I closed my eyes and saw the ver-y rea-son why.

REFRAIN

I saw a man with his head bowed low____ His heart had no place to go, I

looked and I thought to my-self with a sigh:____ There but for you go I. I saw a

man walk-ing by the sea____ A-lone with the tide was he, I looked and I thought as I

watched him go by:____ There but for you go I.____ Lone-ly men a - round me

BRIGADOON

Music by FREDERICK LOEWE

Lyrics by ALAN JAY LERNER

ALMOST LIKE BEING IN LOVE

Music by FREDERICK LOEWE

Lyrics by ALAN JAY LERNER

FROM THIS DAY ON

Music by FREDERICK LOEWE

Lyrics by ALAN JAY LERNER

Moderato

Din-na ye know, Tom-my, that ye're all I'm liv-in' for? _____ So how can ye go Tom-my, when I'll need ye more an' more.

REFRAIN Flowingly

You and the world we knew will glow till my life is through For you're part of me from this day on. _____ And some - - day if I should love it's you I'll be dream-ing of For

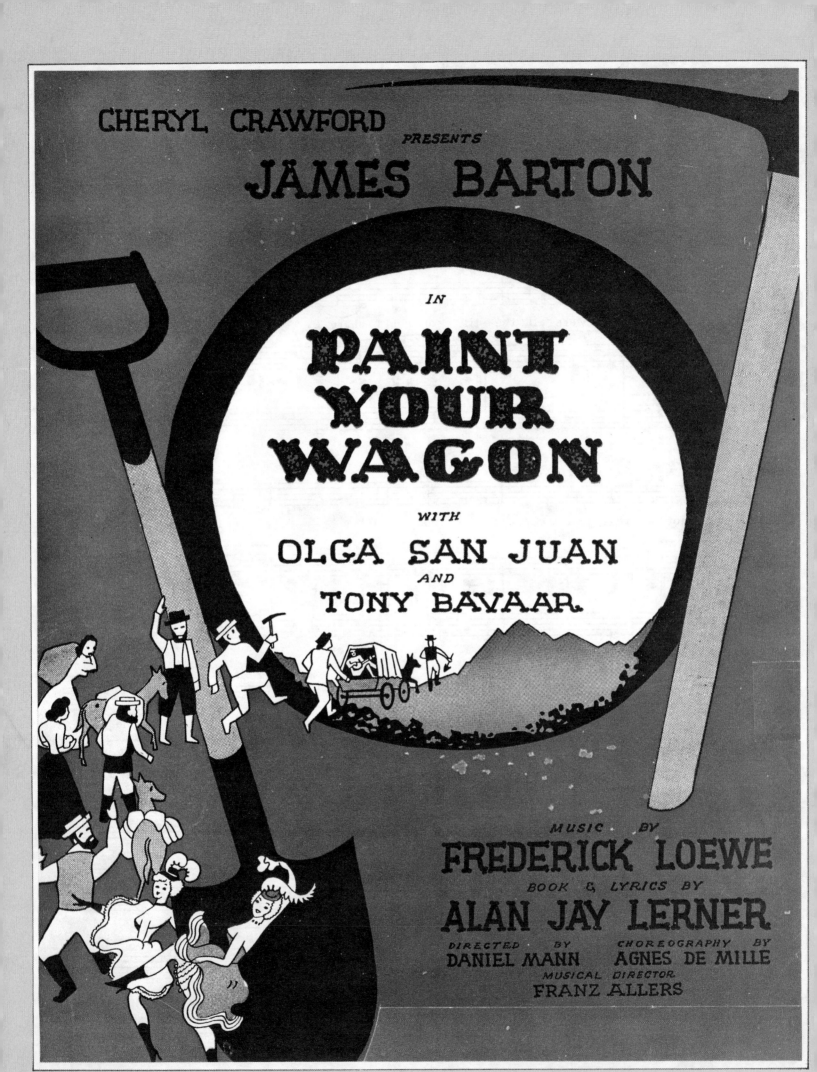

ANOTHER AUTUMN

Music by FREDERICK LOEWE

Lyrics by ALAN JAY LERNER

I STILL SEE ELISA

Music by FREDERICK LOEWE

Lyrics by ALAN JAY LERNER

THEY CALL THE WIND MARIA

Music by FREDERICK LOEWE

Lyrics by ALAN JAY LERNER

I TALK TO THE TREES

Music by FREDERICK LOEWE

Lyrics by ALAN JAY LERNER

I talk to them all _____ in vain. _____

But sud-den-ly my words _____ reach some-one

el - se's ear; _____ Touch some-one el - se's heart -

- strings too. _____ I tell you my

32

WAND'RIN' STAR

Music by FREDERICK LOEWE

Lyrics by ALAN JAY LERNER

34

36

I'M ON MY WAY

Music by FREDERICK LOEWE

Lyrics by ALAN JAY LERNER

39

STARRING **AUDREY HEPBURN · REX HARRISON**

CO STARRING **STANLEY HOLLOWAY** WILFRID HYDE-WHITE GLADYS COOPER JEREMY BRETT

AND THEODORE BIKEL FROM THE BERNARD SHAW PRODUCTION & CECIL BEATON CHOREOGRAPHY BY HERMES PAN MUSIC SUPERVISED BY ANDRE PREVIN

MUSIC BY BOOK, LYRICS & SCREENPLAY BY PRODUCED BY

FREDERICK LOEWE · ALAN JAY LERNER · JACK L WARNER

DIRECTED BY **GEORGE CUKOR** TECHNICOLOR® SUPER PANAVISION® 70 WB®

FILM OPENING OCT. 22, 1964

WOULDN'T IT BE LOVERLY

Music by FREDERICK LOEWE

Lyrics by ALAN JAY LERNER

I COULD HAVE DANCED ALL NIGHT

Music by FREDERICK LOEWE

Lyrics by ALAN JAY LERNER

46

he _____ be - gan to dance _____ with me, _____

I could have danced, danced, danced, _____

all night. I could have night. _____

GET ME TO THE CHURCH ON TIME

Music by FREDERICK LOEWE

Lyrics by ALAN JAY LERNER

OLIVER SMITH'S SET FOR BRIGADOON'S WEDDING SCENE; COSTUMES BY DAVID FFOLKES

BEST MUSICAL OF 1947—NEW YORK DRAMA CRITICS CITATION

BEST CHOREOGRAPHY
AGNES de MILLE
Antoinette Perry Award

BEST LIBRETTIST
ALAN JAY LERNER
Variety Poll

ACTORS' HONOR ROLL
DAVID BROOKS
Ward Morehouse

BEST SCENERY, MUSICAL
OLIVER SMITH
Donaldson Award

BEST COMPOSER
FREDERICK LOEWE
Variety Poll

BEST COSTUMES, MUSICAL
DAVID FFOLKES
Donaldson Award

ELEGANT THIMBLE
CHERYL CRAWFORD
Commonweal Magazine

BEST STAGE DIRECTOR, MUSICAL
ROBERT LEWIS
George Jean Nathan

ACTORS' HONOR ROLL
MARION BELL
Ward Morehouse

BEST DANCE DIRECTOR
AGNES de MILLE
Variety Poll

BEST EXAMPLE OF CASTING, MUSICAL
BRIGADOON
George Jean Nathan

BEST MALE DANCER
JAMES MITCHELL
Donaldson Award

BEST DEBUT PERFOR-MANCE, MUSICAL
MARION BELL
Donaldson Award

BEST COSTUMES
DAVID FFOLKES
Antoinette Perry Award

BEST CHOREOGRAPHER
AGNES de MILLE
Donaldson Award

ACTORS' HONOR ROLL
LEE SULLIVAN
Ward Morehouse

BEST CHOREOGRAPHER
AGNES de MILLE
George Jean Nathan

DANCER OF BEAUTY
VIRGINIA BOSLER
Theatre Arts Magazine

ACTORS' HONOR ROLL
GEORGE KEANE
Ward Morehouse

BEST CHOREOGRAPHY
AGNES de MILLE
American Design Award

BEST FEMALE PERFORM-ANCE, MUSICAL
MARION BELL
George Jean Nathan

BEST FEMALE PERFORM-ANCE, MUSICAL
MARION BELL
Variety Poll

OUTSTANDING MUSICAL COMEDY COMPOSER
FREDERICK LOEWE
Roseland Award

BEST SUBSIDUARY ROLL ACTOR, MUSICAL
GEORGE KEANE
Variety Poll

MOST PROMISING OF NEWER ACTRESSES, MUSICAL
MARION BELL
George Jean Nathan

Dances by Agnes de Mille graced PAINT YOUR WAGON

Johnny Morgan & Jimmy Savo in WHAT'S UP

Clint Eastwood, Lee Marvin & Jean Seberg in the 1969 film of PAINT YOUR WAGON

Above: Audrey Hepburn in the film. Below: Get Me To The Church On Time from the film by Warner Bros.

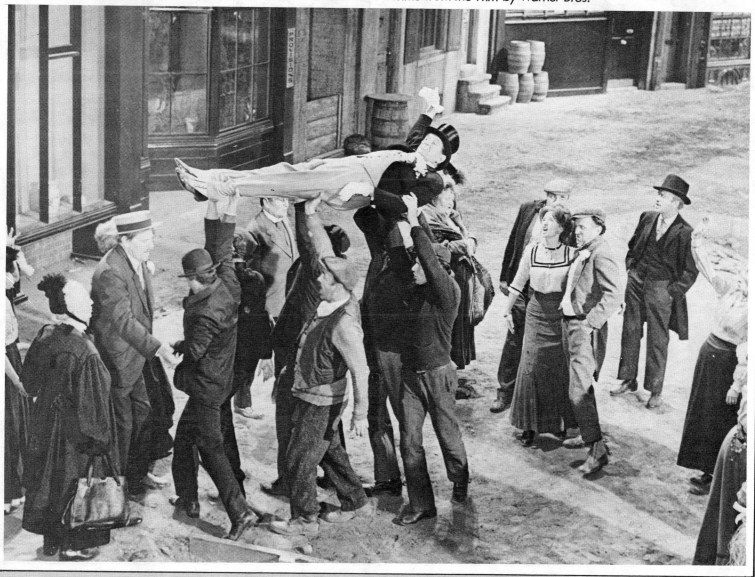

CAMELOT

Richard Burton and Julie Andrews in spectacular CAMELOT

Hermione Gingold, Maurice Chevalier (film)   Below: At Maxim's   MGM's film with Leslie Caron, Louis Jourdan

ON THE STREET WHERE YOU LIVE

Music by FREDERICK LOEWE

Lyrics by ALAN JAY LERNER

That could on-ly be **your** room! _____ This

street is like a gar-den and your door a gar-den gate, _____ What a

love - ly place to wait.

Refrain (slowly)

I have of - ten walked _____ down this street be - fore _____

For there's no-where else on earth that I would rath-er be. Let the time go by, I won't care if I can be here on the street where you live. I have live.

THE RAIN IN SPAIN

Music by FREDERICK LOEWE

Lyrics by ALAN JAY LERNER

WITH A LITTLE BIT OF LUCK

Music by FREDERICK LOEWE

Lyrics by ALAN JAY LERNER

I'VE GROWN ACCUSTOMED TO HER FACE

Music by FREDERICK LOEWE

Lyrics by ALAN JAY LERNER

I've grown ac - cus - tomed to her face _____ She al - most
I've grown ac - cus - tomed to her face _____ She al - most

makes the day be - gin. _____ I've grown ac -
makes the day be - gin. _____ I've got - ten

rene - ly in - de - pen - dent and con - tent be - fore we met;
grate - ful she's a wo - man and so eas - y to for - get;

Sure - ly I could al-ways be that way a - gain and yet, I've grown ac-
Rath - er like a ha - bit one can al-ways break and yet, I've grown ac-

cus - tomed to her looks; Ac - cus - tomed to her voice; Ac-
cus - tomed to the trace of some - thing in the air; Ac-

cus - tomed to her face. I've grown ac- face.
cus - tomed to her face. I've grown ac- face.

FILM OPENING OCT. 26, 1967

CAMELOT

Music by FREDERICK LOEWE

Lyrics by ALAN JAY LERNER

happ' - ly - ev - er - aft - er - ing than here   in
happ' - ly - ev - er - aft - er - ing than here   in

poco rit.   *a tempo*

Cam - - e - lot!
Cam - - e -

accel.   *f*

The   lot!

mf   *f*

rall. e dim.   *p*   *f*

I LOVED YOU ONCE IN SILENCE

Music by FREDERICK LOEWE

Lyrics by ALAN JAY LERNER

FOLLOW ME

Music by FREDERICK LOEWE

Lyrics by ALAN JAY LERNER

HOW TO HANDLE A WOMAN

Music by FREDERICK LOEWE

Lyrics by ALAN JAY LERNER

IF EVER I WOULD LEAVE YOU

Music by FREDERICK LOEWE

Lyrics by ALAN JAY LERNER

Moderato

Piano

mf

f

rit.

Refrain *(with warm expression)*

F9

mp *a tempo*

If ev - er I would leave you____ It would - n't be in

Bbmaj9 Bb Fdim F7 Gdim F7 Bbdim F7(b9)

cresc.

sum - mer.____ See - ing you in sum - mer I nev - er would

Bbmaj9 Bb6 Dm Bb7 Eb Cm F7

p

go.____ Your hair streaked with sun - light,____ Your lips red as

94

THE LUSTY MONTH OF MAY

Music by FREDERICK LOEWE

Lyrics by ALAN JAY LERNER

SAINT-SUBBER
presents
The Los Angeles & San Francisco Civic Light Opera Production
starring

ALFRED DRAKE   AGNES MOOREHEAD
MARIA KARNILOVA
and
DANIEL MASSEY
in
Lerner and Loewe's

GiGi

A New Musical for Broadway

with

KARIN WOLFE as Gigi

GEORGE GAYNES   and   JOE ROSS

TRUMAN GAIGE   SANDAHL BERGMAN   HOWARD CHITJIAN

Book and Lyrics by   Music by
ALAN JAY LERNER   FREDERICK LOEWE

Produced by EDWIN LESTER and SAINT-SUBBER

Scenic Production Designed by OLIVER SMITH
Costumes Designed by OLIVER MESSEL
Lighting by THOMAS SKELTON

Orchestrations by IRWIN KOSTAL   Dance Arrangements by TRUDE RITTMANN

Musical Associate   Associate Dance Director   Production Manager
HARPER MacKAY   MARTIN ALLEN   BILL HOLLAND

Musical Direction by ROSS REIMUELLER

Dances and Musical Numbers Staged by
ONNA WHITE

Directed by
JOSEPH HARDY

ORIGINAL BROADWAY CAST ALBUM RECORDED BY RCA RECORDS AND TAPES

URIS THEATRE 51st St. W. of B'way. Mats Wed., Sat. & Sun.

BROADWAY OPENING NOV. 13, 1973

THE NIGHT THEY INVENTED CHAMPAGNE

Music by FREDERICK LOEWE

Lyrics by ALAN JAY LERNER

The night they in - vent - ed cham - pagne,_____ It's plain as it can be They thought of you and me! The

night they in - vent - ed cham - pagne_____ They

ab - so - lute - ly knew that all we'd want to do Is

fly to the sky on cham - pagne_____ And shout to

ev - 'ry - one in sight_____ That

THE EARTH AND OTHER MINOR THINGS

Music by FREDERICK LOEWE

Lyrics by ALAN JAY LERNER

IN THIS WIDE, WIDE WORLD

Music by FREDERICK LOEWE

Lyrics by ALAN JAY LERNER

GIGI

Music by FREDERICK LOEWE

Lyrics by ALAN JAY LERNER

mi - ra - cle has made you the way you are?

Gi - gi, am I a fool with - out a mind or have I

mere - ly been too blind to re - a - lize? Oh, Gi - gi, why you've been

grow - ing up be - fore my eyes!

THANK HEAVEN FOR LITTLE GIRLS

Music by FREDERICK LOEWE

Lyrics by ALAN JAY LERNER

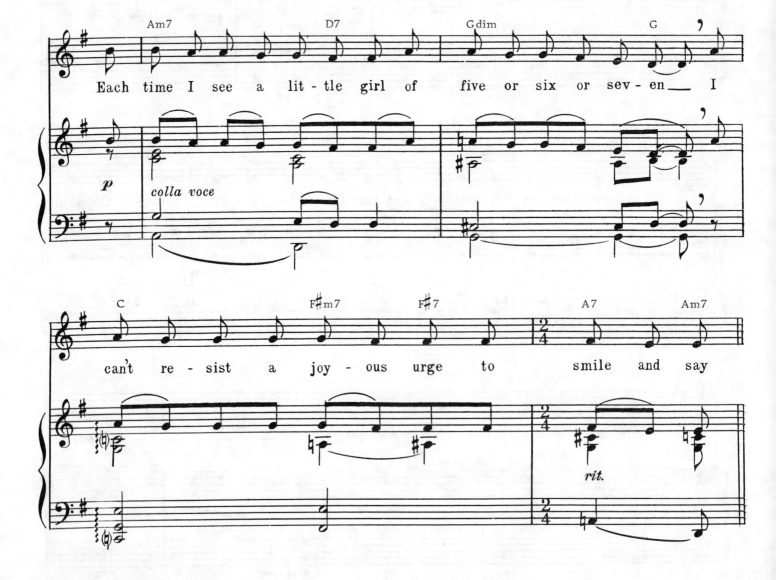

I'M GLAD I'M NOT YOUNG ANYMORE

Music by FREDERICK LOEWE

Lyrics by ALAN JAY LERNER

123

I REMEMBER IT WELL

Music by FREDERICK LOEWE

Lyrics by ALAN JAY LERNER

126

128